God Chasers

FOR KIDS

God Chasers

FOR KIDS

TOMMY TENNEY

Author's note: This book was written using direct quotes and adaptations
from my book, The God Chasers (Shippensburg, PA; Destiny Image Publishers, 1998).

Destiny Image® Publishers, Inc.
P.O. Box 310
Shippensburg, PA 17257-0310

"Speaking to the Purposes of God for This Generation
and for the Generations to Come"

ISBN 0-7684-2165-9

For Worldwide Distribution
Printed in the U.S.A.

This book and all other Destiny Image, Revival Press, MercyPlace,
Fresh Bread, Destiny Image Fiction, and Treasure House books are
available at Christian bookstores and distributors worldwide.

For a U.S. bookstore nearest you, call **1-800-722-6774**.
For more information on foreign distributors, call **717-532-3040**.
Or reach us on the Internet:
www.destinyimage.com

CHAPTERS 1-3: How My Chase Began
1......The Day I Met Him......9
2......The Broken Pulpit......15
3......Forget Your Manners! 21

CHAPTERS 4-8: Bible Guys Who Chased God
4......Moses REALLY Wanted God......27
5......Samuel Learned Early......31
6......David Was a God Chaser; Saul Was NOT a God Chaser......37
7......Uzzah, Uzzah Man......43
8......John the Baptist—Champion God Chaser! 49

CHAPTERS 9-12: God Chasers Yesterday & Today
9......A Puddle of Tears......55
10......Revival at a Police Station......59
11......Touched by the POWER......65
12......Grocery Store Line-Up......71

CHAPTERS 13-15: Up To The Challenge
13......No More Bless-Me Clubs......75
14......Time With Father God......81
15......World Changers......87

Finish Lines......91

A NOTE FOR KIDS FROM TOMMY TENNEY

Did you know that kids have always been important to God? Jesus always seemed to have time for kids, even when other adults wanted them to go somewhere else so they wouldn't bother them.

He loved to talk with them, and He even said that anyone who wanted to go to heaven had to become as a child. I believe that one of the reasons Jesus loves children so much is because they are great *God Chasers*. Children love to be with Him and worship and that makes God feel good.

Are you a God Chaser? This book tells you how I became a God Chaser, and it will help you get better and better at chasing and pursuing the Lord. Put on your spiritual running shoes and join the chase!

Tommy Tenney

Chapter 1

It happened at a church in Texas.

I had preached there several times before but I was in for a big surprise that Sunday morning. Something unusual was about to happen to some God Chasers.

As I walked in to sit down in the front row, the presence of God was in that place so heavily that the air was "thick." You could barely breathe (in a good way, like on a roller coaster ride).

The musicians tried to lead worship, but their tears got in the way. Music became more difficult to play. Finally, they felt God come so close that they couldn't sing or play any longer.

9

The Bible talks about how the "glory of the Lord filled the temple," (see Ex. 40:34; 1 Kings 8:11; 2 Chron. 5:14; Is. 6:1-4) but I'd never understood what it meant. I had felt God come in places, but this time, even after the room seemed to fill up with Him all the way, even more of His presence packed itself into the room!

In the middle of all this, the pastor turned to me and asked me a question. "Tommy, are you ready to start preaching?"

I told him, "Pastor, I'm just about half-afraid to step up there, because I believe that God is about to *do something*."

My pastor friend said, "I feel like I should read Second Chronicles 7:14, and I have a message from the Lord."

With tears pouring from my eyes I nodded and said, "Go, go."

He stepped up to a clear pulpit on the platform and opened the Bible. Then he quietly read the powerful verse from Second Chronicles 7:14: "If My people, which are called by My name, shall humble themselves, and pray, and seek My face, and turn from their wicked ways; then will I hear from heaven, and will forgive their sin, and will heal their land."

Then he closed his Bible, grabbed the edges of the pulpit with shaking hands, and said, "The word of the Lord to us is to stop seeking His benefits and seek Him. We are not to seek His hands any longer, but seek His face."

Right then I heard what sounded like a thunderclap echo through the building!

What happened next changed my life forever.

A GOD CHASER WANTS TO KNOW GOD

READ YOUR BIBLE

If my people, who are called by my name, will humble themselves and pray and seek my face and turn from their wicked ways, then will I hear from heaven and will forgive their sin and will heal their land (2 Chronicles 7:14 NIV).

SAY IT WITH A BEAT:

We Your people,
who are called by Your name,
Will humble ourselves,
and pray, pray, pray—
We will SEEK Your face
and turn from our ways;
We will SEEK Your face
and turn from our ways;
Lord, help me seek Your face…
Help me learn to chase!

Do you know *what "seek" means?* It means to look for, to hunt, to search for something.

TALK TO GOD

"King Jesus, I want to feel Your Presence close to Me. Help me learn what it means to 'seek' You. Amen."

Chapter 2

THE BROKEN PULPIT

My pastor friend was shaking that day when he walked to the platform. While he read that Bible verse in Second Chronicles 7:14, I got up and walked to the back of the room. I knew God was going to do something but I didn't know what or where.

"God," I prayed silently, "I want to be able to see whatever it is You are about to do."

Suddenly, that thunderclap echoed through the building, and at that very moment, the pastor *flew backward* about ten feet!

When he went backward, the pulpit fell forward. The beautiful flower arrangement in front of it fell, and by the time the pulpit hit the ground, it was already in two pieces.

It had split into two pieces as if lightning had hit it!

I quickly stepped to the microphone and said, "I want you to know that God has just moved into this place. Don't worry, the pastor is fine." (It was two and a half hours before he could even get up, though—and even then the ushers had to carry him. We knew he was alive because one of his hands trembled once in awhile. It wasn't a bad thing, he would tell you it was one of the most exciting things that ever happened to him!)

People began to cry because they felt happy and sad at the same time. They were happy because God was so near, but they felt sad because they knew they needed to tell God they were sorry for doing some wrong things. I said,

"If you feel you need to tell God you are sorry, then this is a good time to do it."

I've never seen anything like it. People jumped up and bumped into each other trying to get to the front of the church. They almost forgot their manners! When the people jammed the walkways, other people just climbed over pews! Some of the businessmen even tore their ties off and prayed to God with their faces on the floor.

When I asked the people to come to pray at the front of the church that morning, I had no idea we would do the same thing *seven times* that day.

That Sunday morning service lasted all afternoon, all evening, and into the early morning hours of the next day! (Church is *really different* when God shows up like that.)

A GOD CHASER WANTS
TO BE WITH GOD

Why do you think the pulpit was broken? Was it just because of the awesome power in the room...or did God break it on purpose?

It makes me think about something else that God broke in half—the veil or thick carpet-like divider in the temple when Jesus was alive. It separated people from the Most Holy Place where God's presence was. When Jesus died on the cross the earth shook and the veil was *ripped in half*. Ever since then, God has invited us to come close to Him.

READ YOUR BIBLE

The curtain in the temple sanctuary was split into two parts—from the top to the bottom. The earth shook. Large rocks broke apart (Matthew 27:51).

SAY IT WITH A BEAT

The veil in the temple was ripped in two
So everyone could come to You!
Matthew 27 and verse 51
Fill MY body, MY temple with Your glory, God!
Fill MY body, My temple with Your glory, God!

TALK TO GOD

"Lord Jesus, I ask You to rip in two anything in my life that separates me from You! Fill me up with Your Presence just like you filled the temple in the Bible and just like You filled up that church in Texas! Amen."

Chapter 3

FORGET YOUR MANNERS!

As far as I can tell, there is only one thing that stops God from moving into every church like He did that Sunday in Texas.

Hunger.

Being hungry for God means you really, really, *really* want Him.

Have you ever seen hungry people? I mean *really hungry* people. If you could come with me on a ministry trip to Ethiopia or travel to some other country where people are starving, you would see what happens when sacks of rice are brought. Really hungry people don't wait patiently in line. Really hungry people are so desperate to get food that they forget all about having manners. They don't mean to do it, but they feel too hungry to wait.

That's the way the people were that day in Texas. They jumped up and bumped into each other to reach the front of the church because they were so desperately hungry for God.

Everybody whom I can think of in the New Testament record who "forgot their manners" received something from the Lord. I'm not talking about being rude just to be rude; I'm talking about being so desperate you'll do whatever it takes to get to Jesus! What about the desperate woman with an incurable bleeding problem who shoved her way through the crowd until she touched the hem of the Lord's garment? (See Mt. 9:20-22.) What about the persistent Canaanite woman who just kept begging Jesus to deliver her daughter from demons? (See Mt. 15:22-28.)

The Bible says something very surprising about the Kingdom of Heaven. It says that *"the violent take it by force."* (Mt. 11:12) Have you ever felt that kind of really strong, desperate hunger for God?

It's the kind of ache inside that makes you feel like you REALLY want God to touch your life.

A GOD CHASER WANTS TO CATCH GOD

READ YOUR BIBLE

As the deer pants for streams of water, so my soul pants for You, O God. My soul thirsts for God, for the living God. When can I go and meet with God? (Psalm 42:1-2 NIV)

O God, You are my God, earnestly I seek You; my soul thirsts for You, my body longs for You, in a dry and weary land where there is no water (Psalm 63:1 NIV).

People who are hungry and thirsty for what is right are happy, because they will be filled (Matthew 5:6).

PRAY IT WITH A BEAT

I am so hungry—
Down deep in my soul;
I am so thirsty—
And there's one thing I know—
That nothing in this world
can fill up the hole
To God is the only place
I should go!
I am a God Chaser...
(Taken from the song by Dian Layton,
"God Chasers")

Many people don't realize that the desperate ache they feel inside is really their hunger for God. The Lord is the only one who can satisfy that hunger. When you feel empty and hungry inside, where do you run? Do you try to do something nice for someone to make yourself feel better? Or, do you run to the refrigerator and eat something? Do you run to the television or computer or video game and occupy your mind with entertainment? The next time you feel that empty ache inside try running to God!

Chapter 4

One famous story in the Bible is about the Ten Commandments. You've probably heard it, but have you heard the *sad* part of that story?

God really wanted the children of Israel to come up to the mountain and receive the Ten Commandments *directly from Him* along with Moses. But they wouldn't do it. Do you know why? They were *afraid*.

The Bible says that there was thunder and lightning and the mountain was filled with smoke, so it was a pretty scary day. (See Ex. 20:18, 21.) When the Israelites told Moses that they were scared, he explained to them, "*Don't be afraid. That thunder and lightning is to remind you of God's awesome power so that you won't sin. He loves you, but He just wants you to come clean so He can talk with you.*" (See Ex. 20:20.)

Isn't it amazing how heavy your parents' footsteps sound when you hear them come in your direction *right after you've done something you shouldn't have?*

The Israelites were hearing Father God's footsteps. Moses ran toward Him that day; while calling back to the people, "Come on, guys, it's God. When I was up on the mountain He let me get this close, and now He's *come down* to where you are because He wants *all of us* to come close to Him together. Come on!"

All God wanted the people to do when He gave the Ten Commandments was to do the right things so they could come close to Him. He was tired of looking at them and talking to them from a distance. He wanted to be *close* to them because He really loved them.

Nothing has changed. Did you know that *He still wants to do the same thing* and He wants to be close to *you and me*?

A GOD CHASER WANTS TO BE CLOSE TO GOD

READ YOUR BIBLE

You can read the story for yourself in Exodus 19 and 20.

SAY IT WITH A BEAT:

Exodus 20 and verse 21,
When GOD shows up—
everybody, COME!

TALK TO GOD

"Heavenly Father, You are totally powerful. You are great and awesome and mighty, but You *really* love me too. Help me never to fear Your power. Help me to run close to You, knowing that Your power will protect and keep me safe. I want to hear what You have to say, I want to hear Your voice.

So, Father God, right here...right now...I come. I want to be close to You. Speak to me, Father. I'm listening...."

Chapter 5

SAMUEL LEARNED EARLY

One night an elderly high priest named Eli went to bed. He lived in the tabernacle where the Israelites met with God. The lamp of God was flickering low and was just about to go out, but Eli didn't notice it. His eyes were becoming so weak that he could barely see anything.

Samuel was a young boy who helped Eli serve God in the tabernacle. He was asleep when suddenly he heard someone call his name, "Samuel!" (See 1 Sam. 3.)

Samuel answered, "Here I am," and he ran to Eli and said, "Here I am; you called me." But Eli said, "I didn't call you; go back and lie down." So Samuel went and lay down.

He was nearly asleep when again the voice called, "Samuel!" And Samuel got up and went to Eli and said, "Here I am; you called me." "My son," Eli said, "I didn't call you; go back and lie down."

The voice called Samuel a third time, and Samuel got up and went to Eli and said, "Here I am; you called me." Then Eli finally realized that it was the LORD who was calling the boy.

So Eli told Samuel, "Go and lie down, and if He calls you again, say, 'Speak, LORD, for your servant is listening.'" So Samuel went and lay down.

Then the Lord came and stood there, calling like the other times, "Samuel! Samuel!" Samuel said, "Speak, for Your servant is listening." And

God spoke to young Samuel that night about things that would happen in the future.

There is something sad about this story too. Eli hadn't heard God's voice in so long that when Samuel heard it, he thought Samuel was dreaming! It was like he said, "Go back to sleep. Just keep doing things the way I've taught you to do them, Samuel. It's okay. It has always been this way."

It was as if young Samuel said, "No, it hasn't always been this way! And I'm not happy with it being this way—I want more! I hear something!"

Sometimes the people around you might not be chasing God with all their hearts—don't let that stop you! Young Samuel learned at a very young age to recognize God's voice, and he was a "God Chaser" for the rest of his life!

A GOD CHASER LISTENS FOR GOD'S VOICE

READ YOUR BIBLE

The LORD came and stood there, calling as at the other times, "Samuel! Samuel!" Then Samuel said, "Speak, for your servant is listening" (1 Samuel 3:10 NIV).

SAY IT WITH A BEAT:

Lord, I want to hear
You calling my name
And when You call,
    I'm list-en-ing!
    I'm listening...
    I'm listening...

TALK TO GOD

"Dear Lord, I'm listening. Please speak to me. Right now when I'm young, please teach me to recognize the sound of Your voice. I want to be a God Chaser for the rest of my life. Knowing and obeying Your voice is the most important thing I will ever do, and it's something I can do right now!"

Find a quiet place to listen for God's voice. God speaks to us in many different ways. Sometimes He speaks to us using words or parts of the Bible, but He often uses pictures, ideas, and music too. Listen with your heart to what He will say to you...

Chapter 6

You've probably heard a lot of stories about David. David was young when he began chasing God. He spent hours and hours listening to God and worshiping Him as he watched his father's sheep. David had special experiences with the Lord as a young shepherd boy. With God's help, he defeated lions, bears, and the mighty Philistine warrior, Goliath—even though he was young. (See 1 Sam. 17:37.)

David was God's chosen king, a man who had been prepared all his life by being close to God.

But David was not the first King of Israel. That was Saul, a man who was tall and good-looking. He stood higher than everybody else and he looked like the perfect choice to be Israel's first king. (See 1 Sam. 9:2.) Saul cared more about what the people wanted than about what God wanted. He chased people more than he chased God.

Care more about what God thinks of you than about what people think. David wanted God's approval more than people's approval—he was a God chaser! That is why David was anointed or chosen by God long before he was crowned by the people.

When Saul was King, the Ark of the Covenant was taken from Israel. That means that they lost the Presence of God. King Saul really didn't care about it. Twenty years went by and King Saul never even tried to bring back the Ark of the Covenant. He wasn't interested in chasing or loving God.

David was different. Once Saul was gone and David became King, he wanted more than anything to see God's Presence brought back where it belonged in Jerusalem. He wanted to *live* right next to God's glory. He knew that God's Presence was the only thing in life that really mattered.

God's Presence is the only thing that really matters in *your life*, too.

A GOD CHASER WANTS TO LIVE NEAR GOD

READ YOUR BIBLE

David said: "…Then let us bring again the ark of our God to us; for we did not turn to it in the days of Saul." (1 Chronicles 13:3 NRSV)

SAY IT WITH A BEAT:

I want to be like—David;
He depended on the Presence of God!
I want to be like—David;
I don't want to be like Saul at all!
I don't want to be like Saul!

41

TALK TO GOD

"Lord, every day of my life I will make a choice: I don't want to live that day doing what *I* think is right, I will ask YOU to help me. I don't want to make choices just to make other people like me, I will make choices that will please YOU!"

Chapter 7

Have you ever heard of Uzzah? He shows up in David's story after King David decided that it was time to bring the Ark of the Covenant back to Jerusalem...

They set the ark of God on a new cart and brought it from the house of Abinadab, which was on the hill. Uzzah and Ahio, sons of Abinadab, were guiding the new cart with the ark of God on it, and Ahio was walking in front of it. When they came to the threshing floor of Nacon, Uzzah reached out and took hold of the ark of God, because the oxen stumbled. The Lord's anger burned against Uzzah because of his irreverent act; therefore God struck him down and he died there beside the ark of God. (See 2 Sam. 6:3,4,6,7.)

When David's royal parade came to the place in the road where Farmer Nachon used to shake out the grain from the stalks at harvest time, the oxen pulling the cart stumbled and Uzzah reached out at touched the holy ark thinking he would steady it. Uzzah's name means "strength, boldness, majesty, security." The presence of God never needs *man's strength* to hold it in place.

When Uzzah reached out to steady "God's box" from falling, God seemed to say, "Look, I've let you come this far your own way; enough is enough. If you really want My presence back in Jerusalem, then you're going to have to do it My way."

God had warned the Israelites never to touch the ark, much like parents warn their children never to play with power outlets in the wall. God's

44

power struck down Uzzah right on the spot and stopped David's parade in its tracks.

Some writers think Uzzah grew up around the Ark of the Covenant as a child. Maybe he played on it or sat on it as a kid, and generally didn't think anything about it. If this is true, it was because God's *power* wasn't there during those years.

One of the first things God does when He "turns on the power" in His Church is to bring back a respect for that power.

No one but God knows how the Israelites handled the ark when they first loaded it onto the new cart, but we do know they handled it *differently* after Uzzah died. We know this much: Nobody touched it. Everyone had a new respect for God's glory.

The second time around, David did what he should have done the first time. He found out what God told Moses about moving the Ark of the Covenant long ago. He wanted to know how to do things *God's way*. He found out that God told Moses that only certain Levites, or people from the family of Levi, were allowed to move the ark. Then he called the Levites and gave them a solemn warning…

> *He said to them, "You are the heads of the Levitical families; you and your fellow Levites are to consecrate yourselves and bring up the ark of the LORD, the God of Israel, to the place I have prepared for it. It was because you, the Levites, did not bring it up the first time that the LORD our God broke out in anger against us. We did not inquire of him about how to do it in the prescribed way."* (1 Chronicles 15:12-13 NIV)

I'm not *afraid* of God; I *love* Him. But I now have a *respect* for the glory and the holy things of God that I confess I didn't have before.

How about you? Do you really want Him to come? He *loves you and wants to come close to you*, but you will have to learn how to properly respect the holiness of God.

A GOD CHASER ALWAYS RESPECTS GOD

READ YOUR BIBLE

The fear of the LORD is the beginning of wisdom, and knowledge of the Holy One is understanding (Proverbs 9:10 NIV).

SAY IT WITH A BEAT:

The fear of the Lord
Means to really respect Him,
And that's where wisdom really begins!
The knowledge of God brings under-stand-ing
Look at Proverbs chapter nine and—verse 10!

TALK TO GOD

"Lord God, I respect and honor You. It's just amazing how You even let anyone come close to You...*but You do*!

Right now I kneel before You, Lord Jesus. You are awesome and powerful. You are holy. And I'm REALLY, REALLY glad that You love me!"

Chapter 8

JOHN THE BAPTIST— CHAMPION GOD CHASER!

"Repent! The Kingdom of God is coming! Repent!"

That was the voice of John the Baptist, a champion God Chaser. His voice was heard just before Jesus came on the scene. He helped the people get ready for the Lord's arrival through repentance.

Repentance is a big word, but it just means to *turn around and turn away* from your own ways and follow God. It means to have a change of heart. And when you do that, it's like you build a road for you to get to God (and for God to get to you!). Just ask John the Baptist. When he built the road, Jesus "came walking."

> *During those days, John (the one who immersed people) was preaching in the desert in the land of Judea. He said, "Change your hearts! The kingdom of heaven is very near!" This is the man whom God talked about through the prophet Isaiah: "There is a voice crying out in the desert: 'Prepare the Lord's road. Make His paths straight.' "* (Matthew 3:1-3)

John the Baptist was a very famous and important person, so his followers must have been very surprised when he said, "Jesus must increase, but I must decrease" (See Jn. 3:30.)

Increase means to get larger; decrease means to get smaller. If I decrease, then He can increase. Less of me means more of Him.

John the Baptist understood that the way to be really great is to become a servant; to have everything in your life point toward Jesus and not yourself. Jesus said, "John is greater than any man ever born, but the person who is least important *in the kingdom of heaven* is greater than John." (See Mt. 11:11a.)

Wow.

Do you have plans and desires to really make something of your life? The way to move up higher is to make yourself lower. Give your whole life to Jesus along with all the plans you've made for yourself. His plans for you are *better* than anything you could hope or imagine! (See Jer. 29:11; Eph. 3:20.)

A GOD CHASER MAKES JESUS GREATER

READ YOUR BIBLE

He must increase, but I must decrease (John 3:30 KJV).

SAY IT WITH A BEAT:

John chapter 3, AND verse 30—
This is what John the Baptist said:
"He must INcrease;
I must DEcrease."
HEY!
Make JESUS greater,
and make me LESS.
Make JESUS greater;
and make me LESS.

TALK TO GOD

"Lord Jesus, it sounds hard to do. As a God Chaser, I should make You greater in my life and make my own wants and desires less. I know I'll need Your help again, Lord! Help me to be a true GOD CHASER. Help me to put You and Your Kingdom *first* in my life. I know that Your plans for me are way better than anything I can ever hope, dream or imagine (even though I'm pretty good at it)!"

Chapter 9

Edward Miller wrote a book called, *Cry for Me Argentina*. In the book, Dr. Miller tells about 50 students in his Argentine Bible Institute who began to pray. They prayed so hard that it was impossible to have class! Day after day for 49 days in a row, those students prayed and prayed for Argentina in the Bible school.

Dr. Miller told me that he had never seen people cry and pray so hard for so long!

One young man leaned his head against a wall and cried for other people in his nation for four hours! A trail of tears had run down the wall.

After six hours had passed, he was standing in a *puddle* of his own tears!

Those young prayer warriors cried and prayed day after day, and Dr. Miller said it could only be described as a miracle. The students weren't just repenting for something *they* had done. The Holy Spirit was calling them to repent for the bad things *other people* had done, and for the pain and suffering people felt in their city, their area, and in the country of Argentina.

Because those 50 young people had prayed, the people of Argentina started going to hear people preach about Jesus and heal the sick in soccer stadiums that seated 180,000 people. Even the largest stadiums in Argentina couldn't hold all the people who came!

What about you?

Are you willing to cry and pray to the Lord for people in your country?

A GOD CHASER IS A PRAY-ER

READ YOUR BIBLE

And I sought for anyone among them who would repair the wall and stand in the breach before me on behalf of the land, so that I would not destroy it; but I found no one (Ezekiel 22:30 NRSV).

SAY IT WITH A BEAT:

God's looking for someone to stand in the gap
Who will pray to Him and cry for their land!
That's Ezekiel 22:30; That's Ezekiel 22:30

TALK TO GOD

"Lord, I know that You really, *really* love the people of my country. You want them to turn to You and be saved. Please put the urge in my heart to pray. Give me the strength to cry and pray to You with all my heart."

MAP YOUR PRAYER CHASE

Find that map of your country and lay your hands on it as you pray. Ask God to show you HOW to pray.

- For the government leaders
- For every child in your country
- For every school

Chapter 10

Many years ago, a preacher named Duncan Campbell held revival meetings in the Hebrides (islands near England and Scotland). Some officials from that region came to him very early one morning and said, *"Would you please come to the police station?* There are a lot of people here and we don't know what's wrong with them, but we think you might."

As Duncan Campbell walked with the officials to the police station, it was like something terrible had come on the village. People were crying and praying behind every haystack and every

59

door! Men were kneeling on the street corners and ladies and children in their nightgowns were huddled around each other in their open doorways praying and crying.

When the preacher finally reached the police station, he found a large crowd of people crying out to the police, "What is wrong? What is wrong?"

The people felt like they had done something very bad. The only thing they knew to do was to go to the police station and confess. The police didn't have the answer, and the people didn't know it was God showing them their sins, but Duncan Campbell did!

He stood on the steps of the police station early that morning and preached the simple gospel of Jesus Christ. The people repented to God for their sins and an awesome revival came to that place.

That's the kind of revival I want to see in my town, in your town, and in our whole nation. What we need for revival in America is one thing and one thing only:

We need to have God show up.

A GOD CHASER STAYS CLEAN WITH GOD

READ YOUR BIBLE

Repent, then, and turn to God, so that your sins may be wiped out, that times of refreshing may come from the Lord (Acts 3:19 NIV).

So, change your hearts! Come back to God, so that He may wipe out your sins (Acts 3:19).

SAY IT WITH A BEAT:

Repent!
Repent and turn to God!
Then your sins
will be all gone!
Change your heart
and turn to God!
Acts 3:19—
C'mon! C'mon!

TALK TO GOD

"Lord, I know the feeling I get inside when I've done something wrong. That is when I come to You and repent—when I turn away from my sin and turn to You. I love the way You are so quick to forgive me!"

MAP YOUR PRAYER CHASE

Find a map of your community or city (the phone book will do). Put your hands on it and ask God to show you HOW to pray.

- That people will begin to cry out to God
- For your school
- For people who are in community centers, sports arenas, malls, etc.

Chapter 11

TOUCHED BY THE POWER

Have you ever scraped your feet across the carpet on a fresh cold day and then touched someone? You probably shocked them with a tiny spark of electricity. Electricity generated by your feet rubbing across a carpet creates enough power to produce a little spark, but it takes big generators to make enough electricity to light up a city. The power of God comes in different ways too. He may release enough anointing to produce a little twinge, or His power be so strong that you can't stand up!

I get excited when I read about God Chasers who lived before us and who knew the power of God. William Seymour was a God Chaser who helped spark a great revival in Los Angeles, California at a place called Azusa Street.

Bro. Seymour conducted all-night prayer meetings with other desperate God Chasers and often prayed in humility with his head stuck in the apple crate he used as a makeshift pulpit. God's power descended on those meetings with such intensity that it transformed the lives of men and women of many different races. The news about God's presence (and the fire it ignited) spread around the world.

Smith Wigglesworth was another famous God Chaser from the past. One day a pastor began to pray with Mr. Wigglesworth. This pastor was determined to pray with Mr. Wigglesworth as long as he kept going. In the end, the pastor finally had to crawl out of the room on his hands and knees, saying, *"It was too much of God."* There are many stories about how Smith Wigglesworth carried the power of God with him and worked miracles wherever he went. I call this having a "divine radiation zone."

I don't know about you, but I am tired of just being "another somebody" to the people around me. I made up my mind and set my heart to declare, "I am going to pursue the presence of God in my life." God's presence and glory is *powerful*.

There have been times when God's glory has flowed so much that God Chasers who experienced it had to be careful in restaurants! They might bow their heads to pray over their meal and look up to find waitresses and other customers all around them crying out loud and saying, "What is happening? Who *are* you people?"

This is when people really notice God's people and say, "They have been with Jesus." (See Acts 4:13.) God wants His power and presence to create a divine radiation zone around you that affects everyone who comes near you.

Can the people around YOU tell that you have been spending time with Jesus?

A GOD CHASER KNOWS
THE SOURCE OF ALL POWER

READ THE BIBLE

The Jewish leaders saw that Peter and John were not afraid to speak. They were amazed because they understood that the two men had no education or training. Then they realized that Peter and John had been with Jesus (Acts 4:13).

SAY IT WITH A BEAT:

When people looked at Peter and John
They knew that they'd been with Jesus!
When people look at you and me
Do they know whom we've been to see?

TALK TO GOD

"The more time I spend with You, Lord, the more Your power will fill me up. I want to be so full of You that I become a walking "divine radiation zone" that affects the people around me! I want people to say, "Whoa – that kid's been with Jesus!"

PICTURE YOUR PRAYER CHASE

Put your hands on pictures of each of your family members and ask God to show you HOW to pray.

- For your parents and siblings
- For God's protection and blessing on them
- For the power of God to be in your home and in your lives – that you will each carry a "divine radiation zone"

Chapter 12

My wife, Jeannie, was standing in line to pay for some purchases at a store during the time God was visiting the church in Texas. Someone tapped her on the shoulder and she turned around to see who it was. A total stranger was crying out loud and she didn't care who saw her.

This lady told Jeannie, "I don't know where you've been, and I don't know what you've got. But my husband is a lawyer and we are about to divorce." She tried to talk about some of her other problems, but she finally said, "What I'm really saying is, *I need God!*"

My wife looked around and said, "You mean right here?"

She said, "Right here."

Jeannie just had to ask again, "Well, what about the people in line?"

Suddenly the lady turned to the woman standing in line behind her and said, "Ma'am, is it okay if I pray with this lady right here?"

But that lady was also crying and she said, "Yes, and pray with me too."

If we can carry so much of God's love and glory inside of us that people can feel Him, then we won't have to beg people to come to the Lord in repentance. They will sense how close He is and *run* to Him!

A GOD CHASER CARRIES GOD INSIDE

READ YOUR BIBLE

Make a special holy place in your hearts for Christ, the Lord. Always be ready to give an answer of defense to anyone who asks you why you have hope inside you (1 Peter 3:15).

SAY IT WITH A BEAT:

Always be ready! Always be prepared!
To lead someone to Jesus—
And tell them that He cares!
That's First Peter 3:15;
Jesus, Jesus—live through me!

TALK TO GOD

"Lord, there are people around me every day who are going through hard times and problems. Please help me to help them. I don't want to just think about myself. Help me notice other people and reach out to help them. I want to always be ready to tell someone how special You are and how much You love them."

List the names of three people you know who need Jesus. Pray for them one by one and ask God to *prepare you* to meet with them. Ask Him to help you shine His light into the darkness of their lives. Ask Jesus to be *seen in you*.

_____

_____

_____

Chapter 13

NO MORE BLESS-ME CLUBS

The Lord spoke to me one time while I was ministering and said, "Son, the services *that I like*, and the services *that you like*, are not the same."

I was surprised, but then I began to realize the problem. We really try to make *people* happy and comfortable at church, but we don't try very hard to make *God* feel happy and comfortable there!

At church we often hear people talk about getting "blessings" from the Lord. He does bless us, but have you ever noticed that Psalm 103:1

says, "Bless **the LORD**, O my soul." It does NOT say, "O my Lord, bless *MY soul*."

I wonder if most of us really like God's *presents* (like Christmas or birthday presents) more than we like His presence or nearness. It is really great to want to see God heal people and do miracles, but do we really want to *honor Him*?

Most of the time when we come the church we tell God, "Touch me, bless me, Father," and we make church into "bless me clubs." We shouldn't worry about that because God loves to bless us. We should be mostly interested in spending time with *God the Blesser*!

I travel a lot so I can tell more and more people about God's love and the power of His presence. When I come home to my family after a trip, I don't get very excited if my children meet me at the door asking: "*What did you bring me*, Dad? Did you *get me anything*?"

It is normal for children to get excited about gifts, but what I dream about almost every day I am away is the *love* my children have for me. I can't wait for the moment my six-year-old just crawls up in my lap and "loves" on me with no thoughts about what toy I've tucked into my suitcase.

Father God wishes for the same thing. God chasers want God! They usually don't even think about the "blessings" of God—they just want Him!

Tell Him that you love Him, and every blessing you ever imagined will come to you. Seek the Blesser, not the blessing! Seek His face, not His hands! Don't just get excited about the "toys" that God has; He wants you to be excited about HIM.

A GOD CHASER WANTS GOD MORE THAN ANYTHING

READ YOUR BIBLE

Jesus said: "So, don't worry, thinking to yourself, 'What will we eat?' or, 'What will we drink?' or, 'What will we wear?' People without God put all these things first. Your heavenly Father knows you need all these things. So, put first God's kingdom and what is right. Then all the things you need will be given to you." (Matthew 6:31-33)

SAY IT WITH A BEAT

I won't worry
about my needs—
The King and His Kingdom
are what I want!
Matthew 6:31 to 33;
Matthew 6:31 to 33!

TALK TO GOD

"I'm sorry, Lord. Please forgive me for all the times I've come just to ask You for things. You are my Heavenly Father. Right now I choose to rest in Your arms and tell You that I love You. I'm not bringing you any prayer requests or want lists this time. I just want to spend some time with You because I love You. Besides, You already know what I need."

Chapter 14

TIME WITH FATHER GOD

I love rocking my six-year-old daughter to sleep. Often she will lay back in my arms, and just before she drifts off to sleep she will remember the problems of the day and say something like, "Daddy, this little boy was mean to me on the playground at school," or "Daddy, I had trouble on my spelling test today."

To her these seem like giant problems. I always try to reassure her that everything will be all right in those moments because she is resting in my arms and because I love her. It doesn't matter what anyone said on the playground, and none of her little failures have any power to hurt her because she is in my arms.

Then I get to enjoy my favorite part of the day. That is when my little girl just lays her head back to look at me with her eyes half open and give me her little smile. She doesn't have to speak; I understand. And then in complete peace she drifts off to sleep, with the smile of safety and trust on her face.

That's what our Heavenly Father wants. Some of us come to Him holding so tightly to our problems that we are too frustrated and distracted to see the Father or understand how much He loves us.

What He wants us to do is just *look at Him*. Yes, we can tell Him what we feel. We need to tell Him that, but He is really waiting to receive our trust and worship.

Nothing else is needed. Once God's children lay down their toys and crawl into the Father's lap to seek His face, they will find the peace and comfort that they need.

This is the life of a God Chaser. This is our goal and the reason for our chase—we want to live life in the Father's arms. To live and move and have our very being in Him. (See Acts 17:28.)

So run to Him. Give Him your fears, worries, and problems. Give Him your dreams and your hopes. Then lay back and rest. Your heavenly Father loves you and will take care of you.

A GOD CHASER RESTS IN GOD'S ARMS

READ THE BIBLE

You are tired and have heavy loads. If all of you will come to me, I will give you rest (Matthew 11:28).

SAY IT WITH A BEAT

Matthew 11: 28—
see—Jesus said,
"Come to ME
With all your heavy burdens!
And I will give you rest...Ahh...
And I will give you rest...Ahhhhh...

TALK TO GOD

"Well, here I am, Lord Jesus. I've come to rest in Your arms. You know all about my troubles and fears and problems. I give them all to You *right now*. I belong to You and I trust You to look after my whole life. Thanks for giving me Your rest and peace inside my heart. Ahhhhh…"

Chapter 15

WORLD CHANGERS

The Bible says that God's glory will cover the whole earth. (See Num. 14:21; Hab. 2:14.)

We want God to change the world, but it *begins with us*. If you will let Him, God will make you into what He needs you to be.

You might say, "But how can He change me?"

Well, isn't He the Creator who stepped out on the balcony of Heaven and scooped out the seven seas with the palms of His hands?

Wasn't it God who pinched the earth to make the mountains? Wasn't He the One who turned fishermen into world-changers and hated tax collectors into fearless preachers? He's done it before, and He'll do it again!

The way we are changed is by *spending time with Him.*

Often I see the walkways of churches filled with people who feel as if they have climbed into the lap of the Father. I see them hiding their faces underneath benches and pews as they seek the face of God.

And I say, "Yes! This is it! This is the way the world will be changed. This is the way God's glory will cover the whole earth. It starts right here.

Spend time in His Presence. Choose a time and place where you can pay attention to Him alone. Tell Him how much you love Him (and don't bring out your prayer list). Just allow yourself to love Him and to be loved by your Father God…

And you will be changed.

A GOD CHASER IS A GOD LOVER

READ YOUR BIBLE

But as truly as I live, all the earth shall be filled with the glory of the LORD (Numbers 14:21 KJV).

...It comes from the Spirit of the Lord. With one glory after another, we are being changed to look more like him (2 Corinthians 3:18b).

SAY IT WITH A BEAT

Numbers chapter 14, verses 21—
The earth shall be filled with the glory of God!

TALK TO GOD

"Lord Jesus, I live on the earth and I want You to begin by filling ME with Your glory! Change me and make me into the person You want me to be. Make me more like You as I spend time with You every day."

FINISH LINES

The apostle Paul was a famous God Chaser, and he said, "I press on to win what Christ Jesus won for me. Brothers, I don't think I've already won it, but I'm doing one thing: I am reaching out—forgetting about what is behind me. I am pressing on toward the goal to win the prize to which God called me. It is above in Christ Jesus." (Phil. 3:12-14)

The mark or goal of the race, the highest prize of all is Jesus.

He is the one you are chasing and He will not frustrate you. God will allow you to catch Him. In the same way that a father playing tag allows himself to be caught by his laughing, loving child, your heavenly Father will also allow you to catch Him. Even while you chase Him with your love, your worship, and your prayers, He will suddenly turn and catch you!

Come join the company of God Chasers!

The chase is on....

Adventures in the Kingdom™
CHILDREN'S SERIES
Dian Layton

THE DREAMER
Moira, Seeker's older sister, leaves the Kingdom and disappears into the Valley of Lost Dreams. Can Seeker rescue his sister before it's too late?
0-9707919-4-1 • $4.99p

IN SEARCH OF WANDERER
Come aboard the sailing ship *The Adventurer*, and find out how Seeker learns to fight dragons through the window of the Secret Place.
0-9677402-8-2 • $4.99p

SECRET OF THE BLUE POUCH
The children of the Kingdom explore the pages of an ancient golden book and step through a most remarkable doorway — into a brand new kind of adventure!
0-9677402-7-4 • $4.99p

RESCUED FROM THE DRAGON
The King needs an army to conquer a very disgusting dragon and rescue the people who live in the Village of Greed.
0-9677402-2-3 • $4.99p

SEEKER'S GREAT ADVENTURE
Seeker and his friends leave the *CARNAL*ville of Selfishness and begin the great adventure of really knowing the King!
0-9677402-1-5 • $4.99p

GODChasers.network

GodChasers.network is the ministry of Tommy and Jeannie Tenney. Their heart's desire is to see the presence and power of God fall—not just in churches, but on cities and communities all over the world.

How to contact us:

By Mail:

GodChasers.network
P.O. Box 3355
Pineville, Louisiana 71361
USA

By Phone:

Voice: 318.44CHASE (318.442.4273)

Fax: 318.442.6884

Orders: 888.433.3355

By Internet:

E-mail: GodChaser@GodChasers.net

Website: www.GodChasers.net

Run With Us!

Become a GodChasers.network Monthly Revival Partner

GodChasers are people whose hunger for Him compels them to run—not walk—towards a deeper and more meaningful relationship with the Almighty! For them, it isn't just a casual pursuit. Traditional Sundays and Wednesdays aren't enough—they need Him everyday, in every situation and circumstance, the good times and bad. Are you a GodChaser? Do you believe the body of Christ needs Revival? If my mandate of personal, National and International Revival is a message that resonates in your spirit, I want you to prayfully consider Running with us! Our Revival Partners fuel GodChasers.network to bring the message of unity and the pursuit of His presence around the world! And the results are incredible, yet humbling. As a Revival Partner, your monthly seed becomes the matches we use to set Revival fires around the globe.

For your monthly support of at least thirty dollars or more, I will send you free, personal fuel each month. This could be audio or videotapes of what I feel the Lord is saying that month. In addition, you will receive discounts on all of our ministry resources. Your Revival Partner status will automatically include you in invitation-only gatherings where I will minister in a more intimate setting.

I rely on our Revival Partners to intercede for the ministry in prayer and even minister with us at GodChaser gatherings around the country. I love to sow seed in peoples' lives and have learned that you can't out give God, He always multiplies the seed! If we give Him something to work with, there's no limit how many He can feed, or how many Revival fires can be started!

Will you run with us every month?

In Pursuit,

Tommy Tenney

Tommy Tenney

Become a Monthly Revival Partner by calling or writing to:

Tommy Tenney/GodChasers.network
P.O. Box 3355
Pineville, Louisiana 71361-3355
318.44CHASE (318.442.4273)

Other **God Chaser** Gift Books

Available Everywhere

You Are a God Chaser If... 0-7684-2164-0

God Chasers for Teens 0-7684-2153-5

For a complete list of our titles,
visit us at www.destinyimage.com
Send a request for a catalog to:

Destiny Image® Publishers, Inc.

P.O. Box 310
Shippensburg, PA 17257-0310